Dutch Windmills Quilt

Anne Dease

a **Quilt in a Day**® Publication

I dedicate this book to those who
hold my heart… Jim, Jonathan and
Meghan, and to Mama and Papa
whose courage brought us to this
land of incredible promise.

Published by Quilt in a Day®, Inc.

1955 Diamond Street, San Marcos, CA 92069

Copyright 1995 Anne Dease

First Printing, June, 1995

ISBN 0-922705-87-9

Art Direction, Merritt Voigtlander

Photography, Wayne Norton

Table of Contents

Introduction

There are times, especially after a rain, when the air smells sweeter, the earth richer, that I am strongly reminded of the time I spent in Holland as a child. It is curious what memories seem vivid. I can still picture my Opa (Grandfather) reading quietly from the Bible, while my Oma (Grandmother) sewed diligently on a dress for my favorite doll.

When my parents immigrated to the United States, they worked hard to raise my brother and me with the best of both worlds. I credit my mother with keeping our Dutch heritage alive. To this day we all gather at her home for St. Nicholas, placing our wooden shoes by the fireplace, sing our Dutch songs and enjoy the foods that transport us back to a place far across the Atlantic Ocean.

Of all the gifts we give our children, traditions become the most meaningful. They connect us to a time and place we may no longer frequent, but that we hold close to our hearts. Quilting is a tradition I have passed on to my family. My son Jonathan sleeps under the quilts that I have made him, while my daughter Meghan has proudly made two quilts of her own. My husband and children joined in my excitement as I worked on my latest quilting book.

My parents, Nellie and Theodore Van Klaveren, my brother, Ted and I enjoyed our time in Holland.

My family, including my Opa and Oma Van Roon dressed in traditional Vollendam costumes.

It seemed so fitting that the hearts in the pattern formed a windmill that spun continuously across the quilt. As I stitched each heart, my thoughts continued to go back to fond childhood memories. I feel blessed that my parents chose to raise us in a country so full of opportunity. I am equally proud that my children have continued to participate in the traditions from a homeland far away. I hope generations from now my family will still be cuddling under "Dutch Windmills" quilts. I hope too that this quilt touches your heart as much as it has touched mine. It has been my "Dutch" treat to share it with you.

History

"Dutch Windmills" has a multitude of names. Commonly known as "Hearts and Gizzards," it has also been called "Pierott's PomPom." Some of the names are wonderfully romantic such as "Hearts and Flowers" and "Springtime Blossoms." Other names such as "Tennessee Snowball" are difficult to understand when viewing the pattern.

In a book on Amish quilt history, I saw this quilt design referred to as "Bishop's Quilt." The story goes that when the Bishop would visit a parish member's home, it was considered the greatest honor. It was a time when Amish women would present their finest meals and place their most precious quilts on the bed. Because of the abundance of curved pieces and the expertise it took to construct, this quilt would demonstrate to the Bishop the remarkable skill of the woman who lived in this home. Thank goodness for "Quilt in a Day" and our simplified patterns. Now we can present the finest of quilt designs with a minimal amount of effort!

It was Nancy Cabot who popularized many quilt patterns during the 1930's. Her column in the Chicago Tribune featured quilt designs with an advertisement that the pattern and instructions could be bought through the mail for a nickel! Her version of this quilt was named "Windblown Daisy."

Supplies

- Sharpie™ permanent pen
- Point Turner
- Large rotary cutter with new blade

- Stiletto

Plexiglass rulers

- 6" x 24" long ruler
- 6" x 12" ruler
- 6" square ruler
- 12 ½" Square Up ruler

- Gridded cutting mat
- Gridded pressing mat

For machine quilting

- Invisible thread
- Quilt clips
- Binder clips or masking tape
- Walking foot attachment
- Pinning tool
- 1" Safety pins

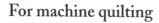

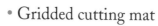

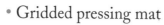

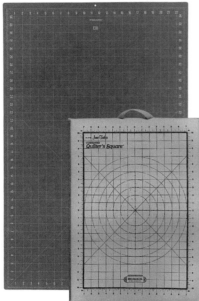

Planning Your Quilt

The "Dutch Windmills" quilt has the simplicity of two fabrics with an option of a simple or mitered border. It is easily made using two different sizes of pieced blocks. The heart shape is traced on fusible interfacing, trimmed from smaller pieced blocks, and fused to the larger block.

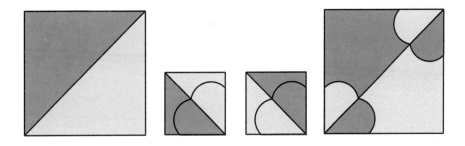

Fabric Selection

Traditionally this quilt pattern was pieced using two solid looking fabrics. The quilt looks best if the fabrics have a strong contrast. The fabrics should be 100% cotton with the yardage at least 42" wide. Be inventive in your choices. If you want to use a patterned fabric, choose one of small to medium scale and be sure its background color does not blend into your second fabric. Directional prints are not recommended. If you wish to use a larger print, you may want to put it in your border as a third fabric, and choose two fabrics that compliment it in your pieced blocks.

Fusible Interfacing

Select fusible interfacing that is nonwoven and of a light to medium weight. One side of the interfacing is smooth in texture, while the other side has fusible dots. **Do not confuse this interfacing with paper backed webbed fusing.**

Miniature Wallhanging

For more of a challenge, you will enjoy making the miniature "Dutch Windmills" wallhanging. You may want to keep your "cut away" heart scraps from your larger sized quilts to use in your miniature quilt.

Paste-Up Sheet

Cut out fabric swatches and paste them in place with a glue stick.

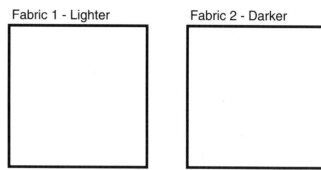

Fabric 1 - Lighter   Fabric 2 - Darker

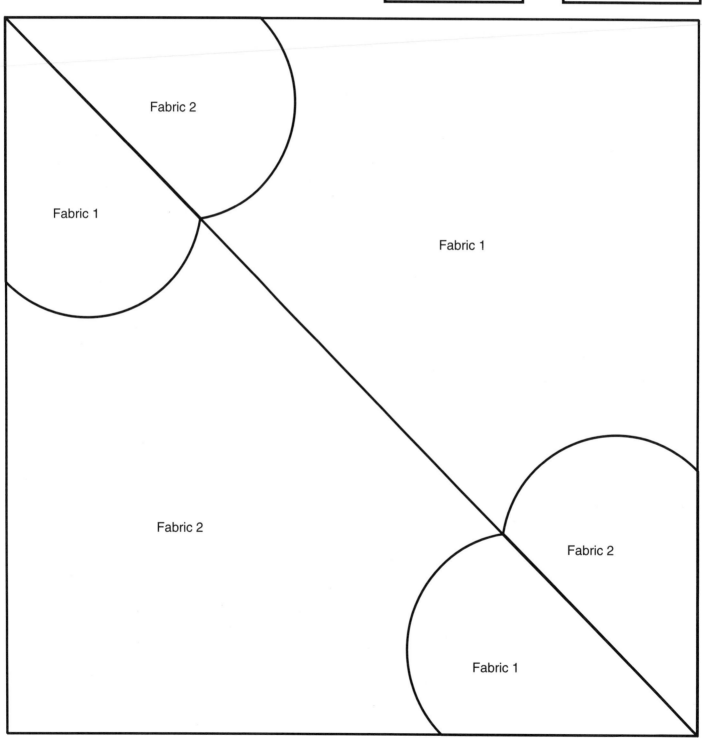

Approximate finished size 8½"

Yardage and Cutting Charts

Baby

16 blocks
4 blocks across
4 blocks down

Approximate finished size 45" x 45"

Yardage & Cutting			*cut strips selvage to selvage*
Fabric 1	1⅓ yds	2	10" wide strips
		3	5½" wide strips
Fabric 2	1⅓ yds	2	10" wide strips
		3	5½" wide strips
Interfacing	1⅓ yds		cut later
First Border	⅔ yd	6	3" wide strips
Second Border	¾ yd	6	4" wide strips
Backing	3 yds	2	equal pieces
Bonded Batting	52" x 52"		
Binding	½ yd	5	3" wide strips

Yardage figured on 42" wide fabric.

Lap Robe

24 blocks
4 blocks across
6 blocks down

Approximate finished size 45" x 62"

Yardage & Cutting			*cut strips selvage to selvage*
Fabric 1	1⅞ yds	3	10" wide strips
		4	5½" wide strips
Fabric 2	1⅞ yds	3	10" wide strips
		4	5½" wide strips
Interfacing	2 yds		cut later
First Border	¾ yd	7	3" wide strips
Second Border	1 yd	7	4" wide strips
Backing	4 yds	2	equal pieces
Bonded Batting	54" x 71"		
Binding	¾ yd	6	3" wide strips

Yardage figured on 42" wide fabric.

Twin

60 blocks
6 blocks across
10 blocks down

Approximate finished size 64" x 98"

Yardage & Cutting			*cut strips selvage to selvage*
Fabric 1	4 yds	8	10" wide strips
		9	5½" wide strips
Fabric 2	4 yds	8	10" wide strips
		9	5½" wide strips
Interfacing	4⅔ yds		cut later
First Border	1 yd	9	3½" wide strips
Second Border	1⅜ yds	9	4½" wide strips
Backing	6 yds	2	equal pieces
Bonded Batting	74" x 108"		
Binding	1 yd	9	3" wide strips

Yardage figured on 42" wide fabric.

Double/Queen

80 blocks
8 blocks across
10 blocks down

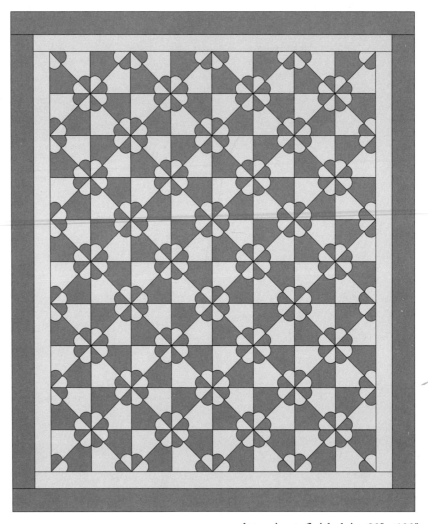

Approximate finished size 83" x 100"

Yardage & Cutting			*cut strips selvage to selvage*
Fabric 1	5 yds	10	10" wide strips
		12	5½" wide strips
Fabric 2	5 yds	10	10" wide strips
		12	5½" wide strips
Interfacing	6 yds		cut later
First Border	1¼ yds	10	4" wide strips
Second Border	1¾ yds	10	5½" wide strips
Backing	9 yds	3	equal pieces
Bonded Batting	90" x 110"		
Binding	1 yd	10	3" wide strips

Yardage figured on 42" wide fabric.

King

100 blocks
10 blocks across
10 blocks down

Approximate finished size 100" x 100"

Yardage & Cutting			cut strips selvage to selvage
Fabric 1	6⅜ yds	13	10" wide strips
		15	5½" wide strips
Fabric 2	6⅜ yds	13	10" wide strips
		15	5½" wide strips
Interfacing	7⅛ yds		cut later
First Border	1½ yds	11	4" wide strips
Second Border	2 yds	11	5½" wide strips
Backing	9 yds	3	equal pieces
Bonded Batting	108" x 108"		
Binding	1 yd	10	3" wide strips

Yardage figured on 42" wide fabric.

Cutting and Sewing Techniques

Cutting Strips

1. Fold fabric, matching the torn edges. The selvages may not match. Lay folded strip on cutting mat with fold on grid line and torn edges extending beyond the first grid line at the left.

2. Lay 6" x 24" ruler on grid line and rotary cut torn edges.

3. Lift and move ruler to the desired strip width.

4. Repeat lifting and moving ruler to cut required number of strips of each fabric.

5. Repeat for cutting other width strips of fabrics and fusible interfacing.

Sewing

Use a ¼" seam allowance and a small stitch, 15 stitches to the inch or #2 setting.

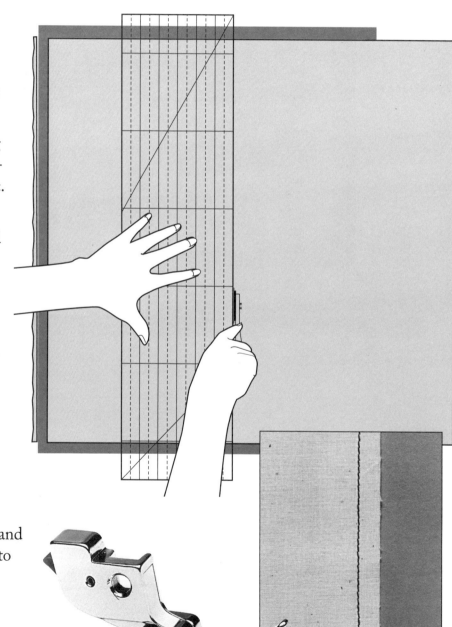

¼" seam

Sewing the Blocks

Making the Large Pieced Blocks

1. Count out this many 10" wide strips of **each** fabric for your size quilt.

Count out this many strips*	
Baby	.2 strips
Lap Robe	.3 strips
Twin	.8 strips
Double – Queen	.10 strips
King	.13 strips

* of each fabric for your size quilt.

2. Lay folded 10" strip on cutting mat with selvage edges extending beyond the left grid line.

3. Trim left end straight. Lift ruler and measure 10". Cut layered squares.

4. Lift ruler, measure and cut at 20". You should get four 10" squares per strip.

   If your fabric is less than 40" wide, cut 9¾" or 9½" squares.

5. Cut 10" squares of each fabric.

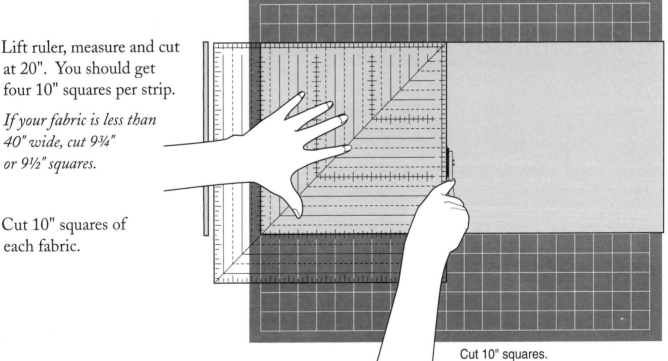

Cut 10" squares.

6. Stack each fabric right side up.

7. Compare the wrong sides and choose one stack that shows a pencil mark better. Turn that stack wrong side up.

8. Lay out that square wrong side up. Lay a 6" x 24" ruler from corner to corner. Draw a pencil line across the wrong side of the squares in that stack.

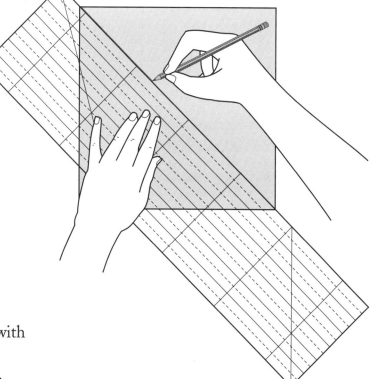

9. Place a marked square right sides together with an unmarked square.

10. Press and pin on both sides of the marked line.

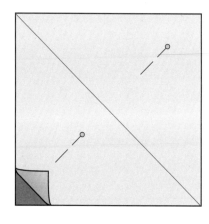
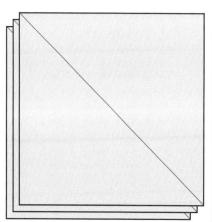

11. Using 15 stitches to the inch, sew an accurate ¼"
    from the marked line. Do not cut threads.

12. Assembly-line sew remaining paired squares.

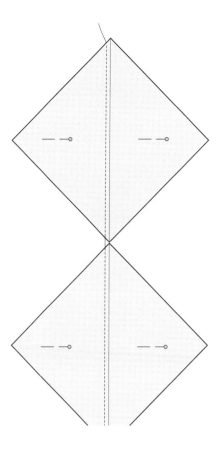

13. Remove from the machine and turn chain
    around to sew on the other side of the line.

14. Carefully cut connecting threads and stack.

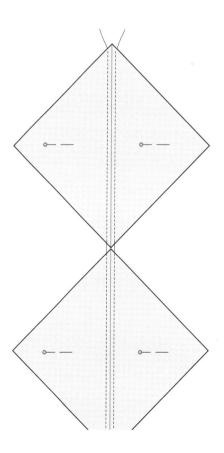

15. Press the squares.

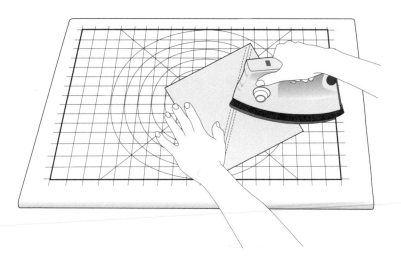

16. Lay square on cutting mat. Cut on the line.

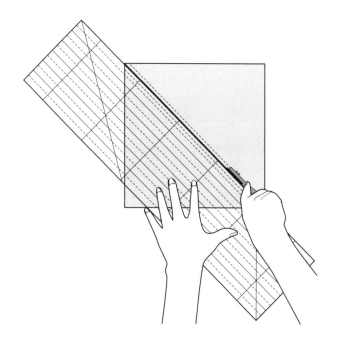

17. Place triangle on pressing mat with darker fabric on top. Press triangles open. The seam allowance will lie under the darker fabric.

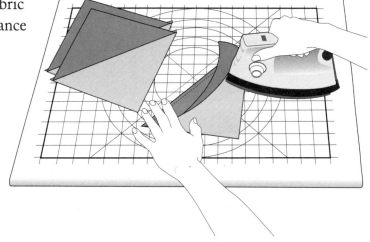

Squaring the Blocks to Nine Inches

1. Place the upper right corner of the 12½" Square Up ruler on top of the block with its 45 degree line on the diagonal seam. Shift the ruler along the diagonal line. Ruler should cover 9" square area.

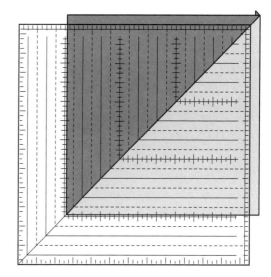

2. Trim irregular edges on two exposed sides.

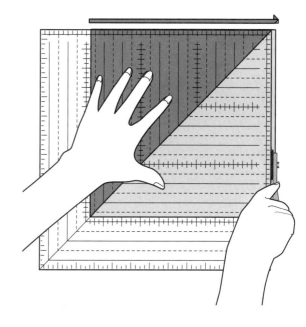

3. Turn the block in the opposite direction.

4. Trim the two remaining sides to an accurate 9" square.

5. Repeat with remaining blocks.

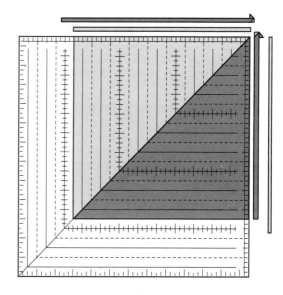

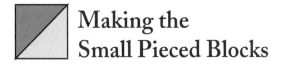 # Making the Small Pieced Blocks

1. Count out this many 5½" wide strips of **each** fabric.

* of each fabric for your size quilt.

2. Lay folded 5½" strip on cutting mat with selvage end extending beyond the left grid line.

3. Trim left end straight.

4. Lift ruler and measure over 5½".

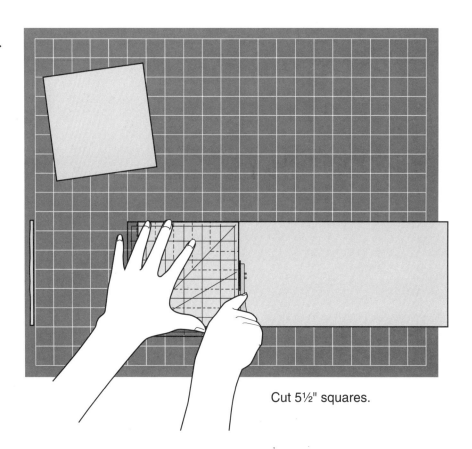

Cut 5½" squares.

5. Cut 5½" squares. You may layer cut more than one folded strip.

6. Stack each fabric right side up.

7. Compare the wrong sides and choose one stack to mark. Turn that stack wrong side up.

8. Lay out a square wrong side up.

9. Lay 6" x 12" ruler from corner to corner. Draw a line.

10. Mark all squares in that stack.

11. Place a marked square right sides together with an unmarked square.

    Press and pin on both sides of the marked line.

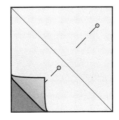 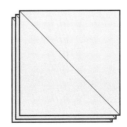 

12. Using 15 stitches to the inch, sew an accurate ¼" from the marked line.

Do not cut threads. Assembly-line sew remaining paired squares.

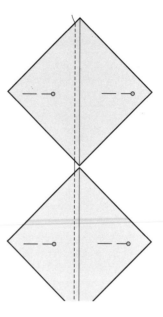

13. Remove from the machine. Turn chain around and sew on the other side of the line.

14. Carefully cut connecting threads and stack.

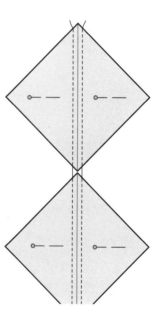

15. Press squares.

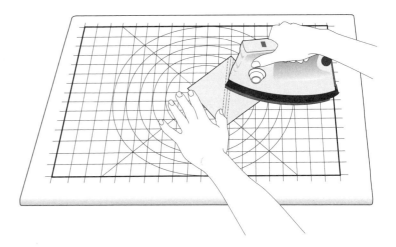

16. Lay square on cutting mat. Cut on the line.

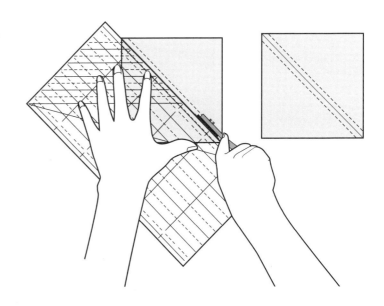

17. Press triangles open. The seam allowance
    will lie under the darker fabric.

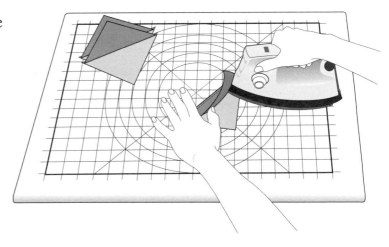

Squaring the Small Blocks

Measure the blocks to find an average measurement. This should be between 4¾" - 5".
Square all of the blocks to your
average measurement.

1. Place the upper right corner of the 6" x 6" ruler
   on top of the block with its 45 degree line on
   the diagonal seam. Shift the ruler along the
   diagonal line. Ruler should cover the area of
   your measurement.

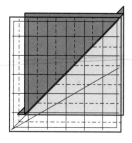

2. Trim irregular edges on two exposed sides.

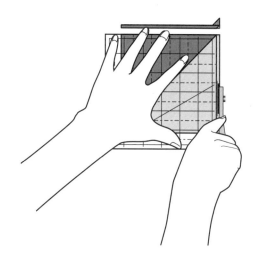

3. Turn the block in the opposite direction.
   Trim the two remaining sides to your
   average measurement.

4. Repeat with remaining blocks.
   Stack right side up.

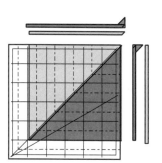

Cutting Fusible Interfacing Squares

Fusible interfacing is based on 22" wide yardage.

1. Use your size of the small block as the width of the interfacing strips. (4¾" or 5")

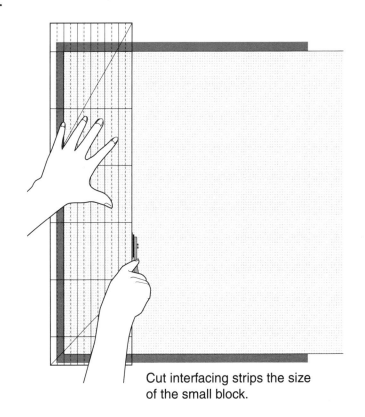

Cut interfacing strips the size of the small block.

Cut this many strips

Baby . . . . 8 strips

Lap Robe . . . . 12 strips

Twin. . . . . 30 strips

Double – Queen . . . . . . 40 strips

King . . . . 50 strips

2. Cut this number of squares of interfacing for your size quilt. Stack smooth side up.

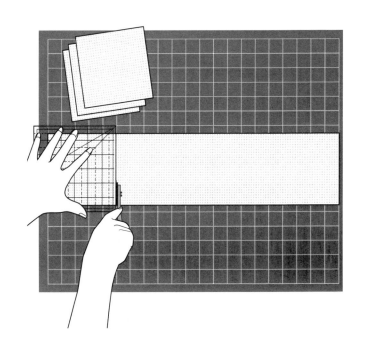

Cut this many squares

Baby . . . . 32 squares

Lap Robe. . . . . 48 squares

Twin . . . . 120 squares

Double – Queen . . . . 160 squares

King . . . . 200 squares

Making the Template

A template is a durable pattern that can be used over and over again. Template plastic is excellent for this purpose. Lay clear or opaque template plastic over the paper pattern, found on page 49. Trace the pattern, very carefully. Cut out the template very accurately on the marked line. The seam allowance is included.

A template printed on template plastic has been provided for your convenience in the back of the book.

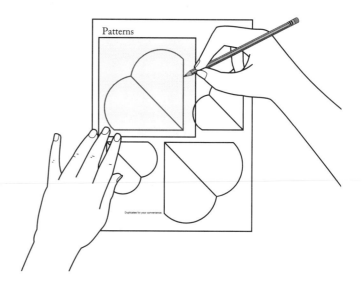

Marking the Interfacing

1. Lay out a square of **interfacing smooth side up**. Lay the template on top of a square of interfacing.

2. Trace the curves of the template with a fine line permanent pen, making sure to mark dark enough to be seen easily against the darker fabric.

   Since this is a sewing line, be careful to use a permanent marker that won't run when ironed or washed. Pre-test your marker for running on a piece of scrap fabric.

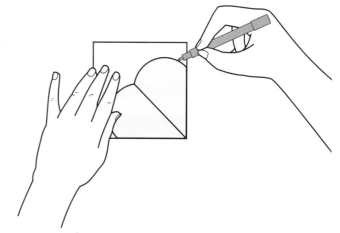

3. With a small ruler, draw the straight line.

4. Repeat for all interfacing squares.

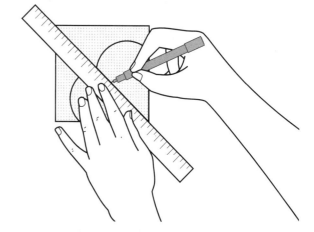

Preparing to Applique

1. Divide the small pieced squares into two equal stacks. Lay out stacks. Be sure they match the illustration.

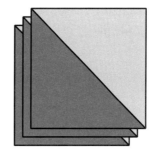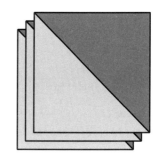

2. Place the marked interfacing on top of the fabric square with the **smooth side of the interfacing on top**. Be sure the center of the heart is placed accurately on the diagonal line of the fabric square, and the edges match.

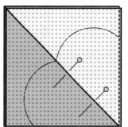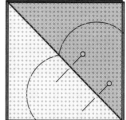

3. Pin to secure the interfacing to fabric square. Stack.

4. Place an open toed, metal foot on your sewing machine.

5. Using 20 stitches to the inch or 1.5 setting, stitch on the inside edge of the marked line of the template. When you come to the center of the heart, place your needle in the fabric on the stitching line, lift the presser foot, pivot the fabric, put the presser foot back down, and continue sewing. Stitch evenly on the curved edges.

6. Repeat for all of the hearts.

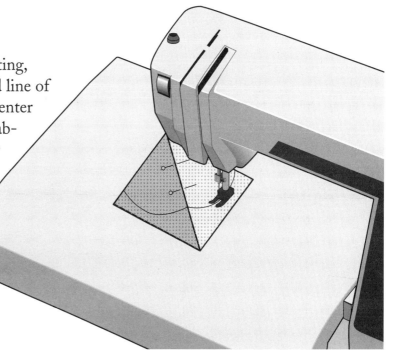

7. Trim away the seam allowance to ⅛". Clip at the center of the heart, being careful not to cut to the stitching.

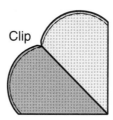

8. Turn right side out, smoothing the heart with the rounded edge of your point turner.

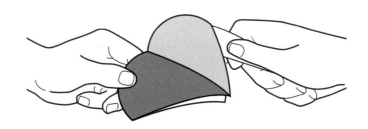

Do not press yet!

9. Crease curved edges with point turner.

Appliqueing the Hearts onto the Large Block

1. Place a heart on each diagonal corner of a larger block. Be sure that the heart fabrics are lying on the opposite fabrics of the large blocks.

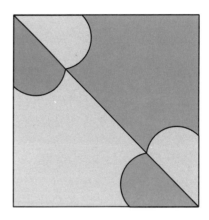

2. Press into place using a heavy iron on a cotton setting. Use steam.

   If your iron is not hot enough to fuse the hearts, press the blocks on aluminum foil with the shiny side up, or on a teflon™ pressing cloth.

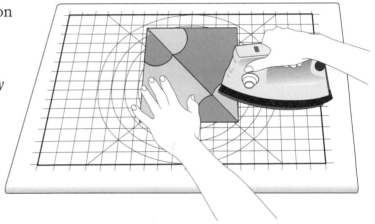

3. Pin across seam and stack.

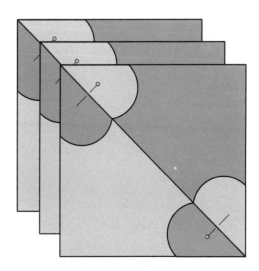

Invisible Applique Technique

Sewing the heart to the large block

Check the needle to make sure it is sharp.
Use a #70 or #10 needle.

Set the Blind Hem Stitch on your machine.

If your machine does not have a Blind Hem
Stitch, or if the Blind Hem Stitch catches to the
right instead of to the left, use a regular zigzag
stitch or blanket stitch.

Set the stitch width to approximately 1½.

The stitch length varies with different machines:
set the stitch length to approximately 2 for
European machines, or 15 stitches per inch for
American machines.

Thread the invisible nylon thread on the top.
Loosen the top tension. Continue to use regular
thread in the bobbin.

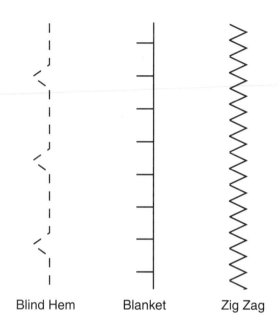

Blind Hem   Blanket   Zig Zag

1. Sew closely around the outside edge of the heart
   on the background fabric. It is important that
   one of the catching stitches falls within the first
   and last ¼" of the heart.

   Pivot with the needle in the fabric at the center
   of the heart.

2. Repeat for each heart.

3. Press blocks lightly and stack.

   Option: For an "old fashioned look," use regular
   thread on top and in the bobbin with the
   blanket stitch. Quiltmakers from the
   1930's often used black thread.

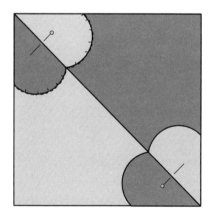

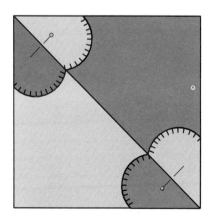

Removing Interfacing and Block Portion Under Heart

Removing these layers reduces the bulk where the corner seams meet.

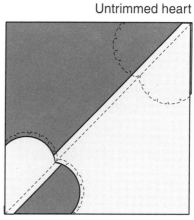

Untrimmed heart

Trimmed heart

1. Gently lift corner of heart and peel back interfacing and block background. Use rounded corner of point turner to loosen curved edges.

2. From the back, carefully trim away excess interfacing and block background leaving a ¼" seam allowance along the curves.

   Be careful not to cut into stitching lines.

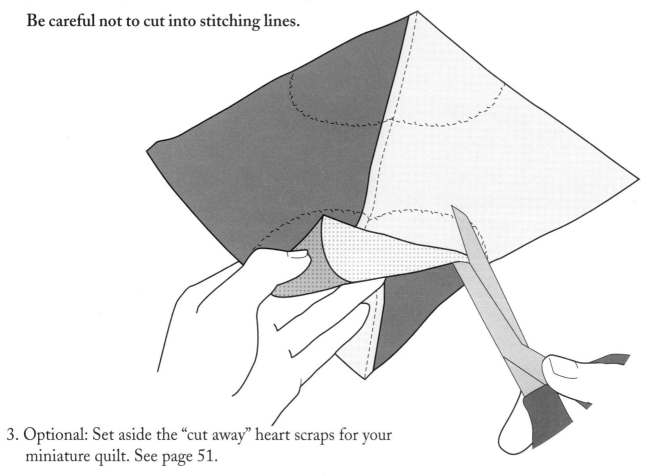

3. Optional: Set aside the "cut away" heart scraps for your miniature quilt. See page 51.

Sewing the Blocks Together

Sewing the Blocks into Pairs

1. Divide the blocks into 2 equal stacks.

   Arrange each stack consistently.
   Stack this many blocks in each:

Stack this many blocks	
Baby	.8 blocks
Lap Robe	.12 blocks
Twin	.30 blocks
Double – Queen	.40 blocks
King	.50 blocks

2. Flip the top blocks right sides together.

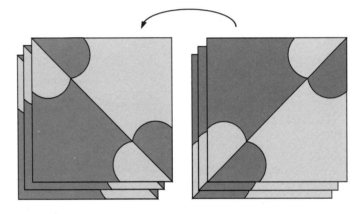

   Pin seams where the hearts will connect
   in the blocks.

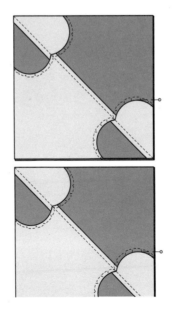

3. Sew the first pair using a stiletto to keep seams flat. Do not cut thread. Butt on the second pair and assembly-line sew stacks.

4. Remove from machine. Clip connecting threads.

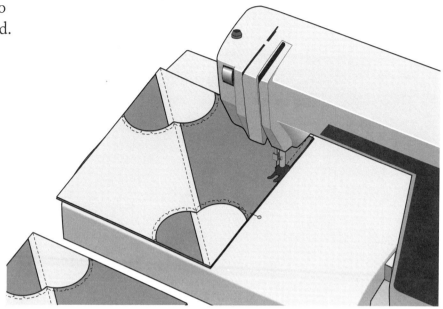

5. Press seam allowance to the darker fabric.

   Lay the pair of unopened blocks on the pressing mat with the darker fabric at the seam away from you. Press the stitching to "set the seam."

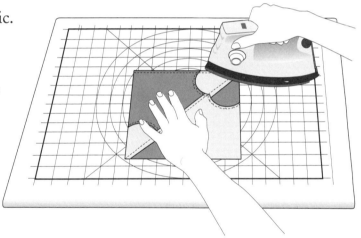

   Lift the upper block and press toward the seam, pushing the seam allowance toward the dark part of the upper block. Press all pairs in this manner.

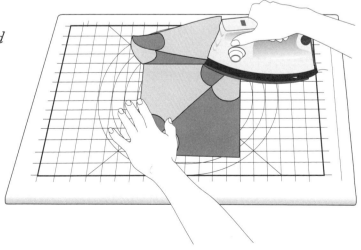

Sewing the Pairs into Sets of Four

1. Lay out the pairs into sets of four with the heart blocks forming a wreath in the center.

2. Sew the pairs into sets of four.

3. Lay the set of unopened blocks, seam away from you on the pressing mat.

4. Set the seam. Lift the upper blocks, and press seam.

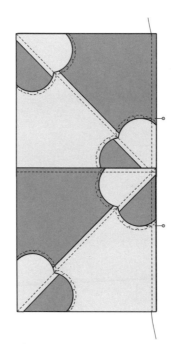

Sewing the Sets Together

1. Following the design for your size quilt, sew sets into horizontal rows. Pin where the hearts will connect in the blocks.

2. Press those vertical seams all in one direction.

3. Continue sewing horizontal rows.

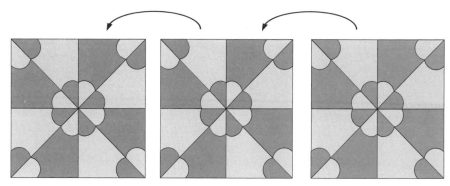

4. Alternate pressing in each row so vertical seams interlock with the row above.

5. Continue for as many rows for your size quilt.

6. Sew the rows together.

7. Press horizontal seams in either direction.

Adding the Borders

Designing the Borders

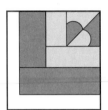 Two border options are given for the "Dutch Windmills" quilt—a Simple Border and a Mitered Border. You will have extra strips if you choose the Simple Border. The Mitered Border is the more advanced and begins on page 39.

You may wish to custom design the border; however, this may change both your border yardage and the amount of fabric needed for the backing and batting.

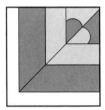 When custom fitting your quilt, lay the quilt on your bed before adding the border and backing. Measure to find how much border is needed to get the fit that you want. Keep in mind that the quilt will "shrink" approximately 3" in the length and width after machine quilting.

Piecing the Strips for Simple or Mitered Border and Binding

1. Stack and square off the ends of each strip, trimming away the selvage edges.

2. Seam the strips of each fabric into one long piece by assembly-line sewing.

   Lay the first strip right side up. Lay the second strip right sides to it. Backstitch, stitch the short ends together, and backstitch again.

   Take the strip on the top and fold it so the right side is up. Place the third strip right sides to it, backstitch and stitch, and backstitch again.

3. Clip the threads holding the strips together.

4. Press seams to one side.

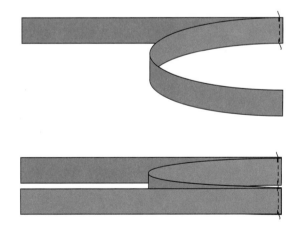

Simple Border

1. Measure down the center of the quilt to find the length. Cut two strips that measurement plus two inches.

2. Right sides together, match and pin the center of the strips to the center of the sides. Extend one inch of strip on each end. Be sure to pin at the ends and intermittently along the sides.

4. Sew ¼" seam allowance with the quilt on top.

5. Press, directing the seams toward the border.

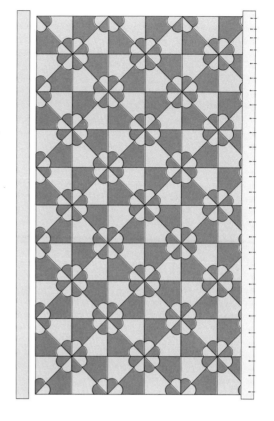

6. Square the ends even with the top and bottom edges of the quilt.

7. Measure the width across the center including the newly added border. Cut two strips that measurement plus two inches.

8. Right sides together, match and pin the center of the strips to the center of the top and bottom edges of the quilt. Extend one inch of strip on each end. Pin at the ends and along the width of the border.

9. Sew with the quilt on top.

10. Press, directing the seams toward the border.

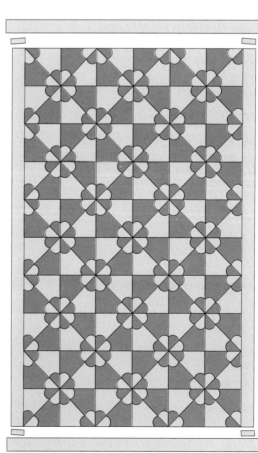

11. Square the ends even with the side borders.

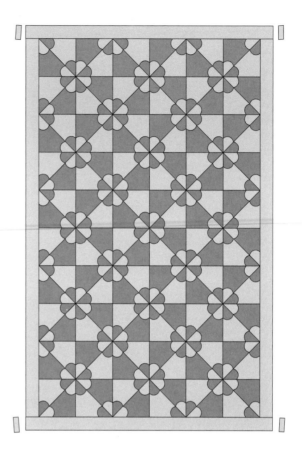

12. Repeat with each border.

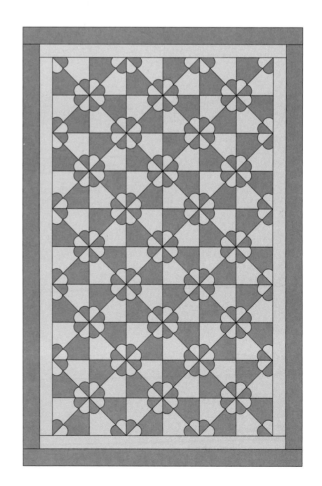

Mitered Border

The Mitered Border option is for the more advanced quilter. This border enhances your quilt by carrying out the diagonal line of the hearts into the border design.

Sewing the Border Strips Together Before Mitering

1. Sew both long border strips together lengthwise. Vertical seams may or may not meet depending on fabric widths.

2. Press the seam allowance to the second border.

3. Measure the width of the two borders.

Width of
your borders [ ]

Measuring your Quilt

1. Measure the width of the quilt. [ ]

2. Measure the length of the quilt. [ ]

Square quilts will have equal width and length.

Cutting the Border for the Width of the Quilt

To determine how long to cut the border strips for the width, use the following formula:

Width of
the Quilt + [ ]

Width of
the borders + [ ]

Width of
the borders + [ ]

add 5" + [5"]

Length of
Strips = [ ]

From the pieced border strip, cut two pieces for the top and bottom.

Example of Twin

Marking the Quilt Corners

At each corner of the quilt, mark a dot on the wrong side ¼" from the edges. The dot will be on the diagonal seam of the block.

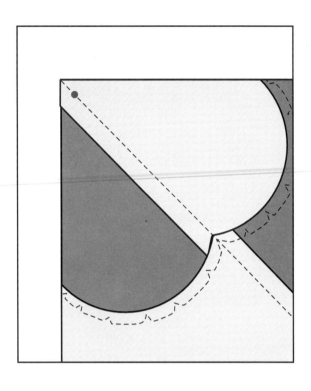

Sewing the Top and Bottom Borders to Your Quilt

1. Fold to find the center of the border strip. Match it to the center of the top of the quilt.

2. Right sides together pin at the center point and along the length of the border strip, stopping with a pin in the marked ¼" dot. Allow the extra length to hang over equally on each end.

3. With the quilt on top and the border underneath, place your needle down in the ¼" dot. Take a single backstitch, then sew forward along the length of the border strip. Stop sewing at the pin marking the ¼" dot at the opposite end, taking a single backstitch to secure.

4. Repeat for the other side.

5. Press seam toward the border

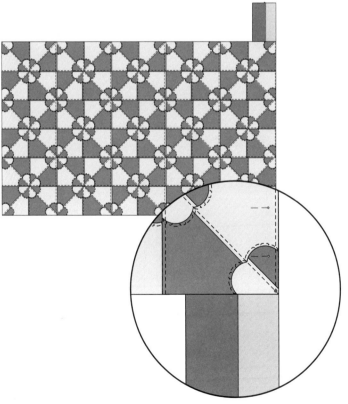

Cutting the Borders for the Length of the Quilt

To determine how long to cut the border strips for the length, use the following formula:

Length of the Quilt	+	
Width of the borders	+	
Width of the borders	+	
add 5"	+	5"
Length of Strips	=	

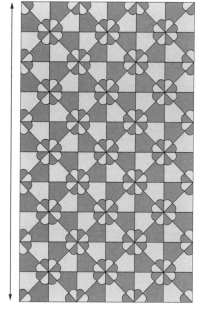

Example of Twin

From the pieced border strip, cut two pieces for the sides.

Sewing the Side Borders to Your Quilt

1. Pull the top and bottom borders out of the way.

2. Find the center of the side border strip and match it to the center of the long side of the quilt.

3. Right sides together, pin at the center point and along the length of the border strip, stopping with a pin in the marked ¼" dot. Allow the extra length to hang over equally on each end.

4. With the quilt on top and border underneath, place your needle down in the ¼" dot. Take a single back-stitch, then sew forward along the length of the border strip. Stop sewing at the pin marking the ¼" dot at the opposite end, taking a single backstitch to secure.

5. Repeat for the other long side.

6. Press seams toward the border.

Sewing the Mitered Corners

1. Fingerpress both seam allowances toward the quilt top to expose the stitching.

2. Line up the 45 degree line on the 6" x 24" ruler with the border seam and the ¼" dot.

3. Following the fold of the quilt and the 45 degree line, lightly draw a diagonal line on the border extension from the ¼" dot. Pin.

4. Beginning exactly at the ¼" dot, take a stitch, a single backstitch and then sew directly on the drawn line.

6. Check the miter from the right side. Redo if necessary.

7. Trim away the excess border ¼" from the stitched line.

8. Press the seam open.

9. Repeat at each corner.

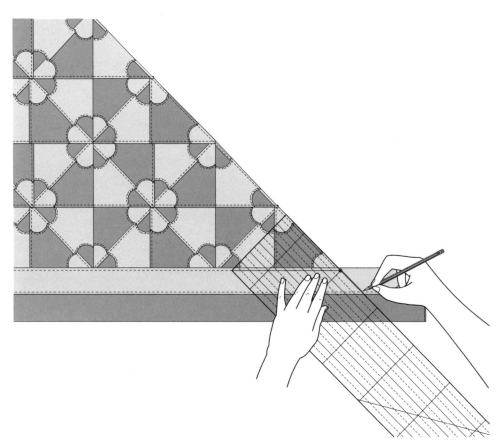

Machine Quilting

Layering Quilt Top with Backing and Batting

1. Piece the backing yardage together for larger size quilts.

2. Stretch out the backing right side down on a large floor area or table. Tape down on a floor area or clamp onto a table with large binder clips.

3. Place and smooth out the batting on top. Lay the quilt top right side up and centered on top of the batting. Completely smooth and stretch all layers until they are flat. Re-tape or clip securely. The backing and batting should extend at least 2" on all sides.

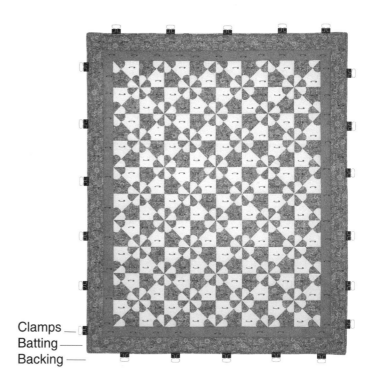

Clamps —
Batting —
Backing —

Quick and Easy Safety Pinning

1. Place 1" safety pins throughout the quilt away from the seams.

2. Begin pinning in the center and work to the outside, spacing them in the center of every "triangle."

Grasp the opened pin in your right hand and the pinning tool in your left hand. Push the pin through the three layers, and bring the tip of the pin back out. Catch the tip in the groove of the tool and allow point to extend far enough to push pin closure down.

Machine Quilting the Straight Lines

Use a walking foot attachment for the straight line quilting. Use invisible thread in the top of your machine and regular thread in the bobbin to match the backing. Loosen the top tension, and lengthen your stitch to 8 - 10 stitches per inch, or a #3 or #4 setting.

1. Roll the quilt tightly from the outside edge in toward middle. Hold this roll with quilt clips or pins.

2. Slide this roll into the keyhole of the sewing machine.

3. Place the needle in the depth of the seam and pull up the bobbin thread. Lock your thread with ½" of tiny stitches when you begin and end your sewing line. Run your hand underneath to feel for puckers.

4. Place your hands flat on both sides of the needle. Keep the quilt area flat and tight. If you need to ease in the top fabric, feed the quilt through the machine by pushing the layers of fabric and batting forward underneath the walking foot.

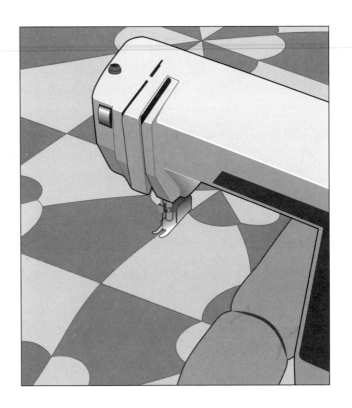

5. Unroll, roll, and machine quilt on all straight lines, sewing the length, width, and/or diagonal of the quilt.

If puckering occurs, remove the stitching by grasping the bobbin thread with a pin or tweezers and pull gently to expose the invisible thread. Touch the invisible thread stitches with the rotary cutter blade as you pull the bobbin thread free from the quilt. Re-sew.

Straight Line
Machine Quilting

Horizontal & Vertical

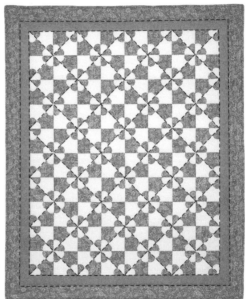

Diagonal

Horizontal, Vertical
& Diagonal

Adding the Binding

Use a walking foot attachment and regular thread on top and in the bobbin to match the binding. Use 10 stitches per inch, or #3 setting.

See page 36 to make one long binding strip.

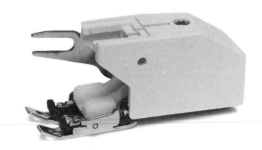

1. Press the binding strip in half lengthwise with right sides out.

2. Line up the raw edges of the folded binding with the raw edge of the quilt top at the middle of one side.

3. Begin sewing 4" from the end of the binding.

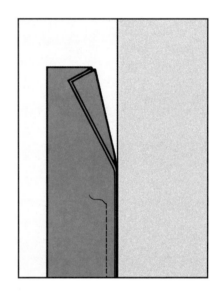

4. At the corner, stop the stitching ¼" from the edge with the needle in the fabric. Raise the presser foot and turn the quilt to the next side. Put the foot back down.

5. Sew backwards ¼" to the edge of the binding, raise the foot, and pull the quilt forward slightly.

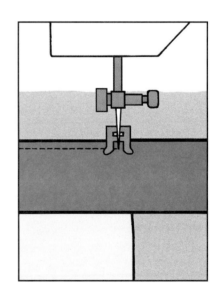

6. Fold the binding strip straight up on the diagonal. Fingerpress in the diagonal fold.

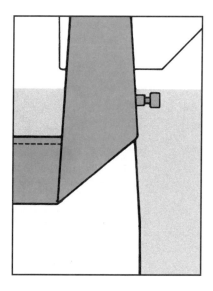

7. Fold the binding strip straight down with the diagonal fold underneath. Line up the top of the fold with the raw edge of the binding underneath.

8. Begin sewing from the corner.

9. Continue sewing and mitering the corners around the outside of the quilt.

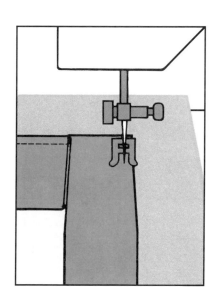

10. Stop sewing 4" from where the ends will overlap.

11. Line up the two ends of binding. Trim the excess with a ½" overlap.

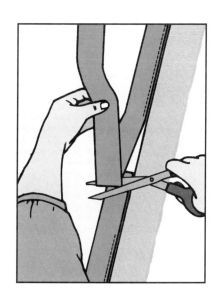

12. Open out the folded ends and pin right sides together. Sew a ¼" seam.

13. Continue to sew the binding in place.

14. Trim the batting and backing up to the raw edges of the binding.

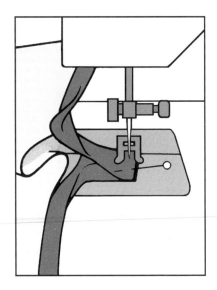

15. Fold the binding to the backside of the quilt. Pin in place so that the folded edge on the binding covers the stitching line. Tuck in the excess fabric at each miter on the diagonal.

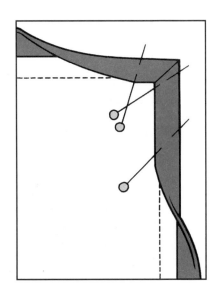

16. From the right side, "stitch in the ditch" using invisible thread on the right side, and a bobbin thread to match the binding on the back side. Catch the folded edge of the binding on the back side with the stitching.

17. Sew an identification label on the backing.

    Optional: Slipstitch the binding in place by hand.

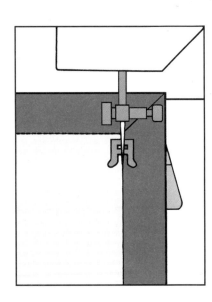

Patterns

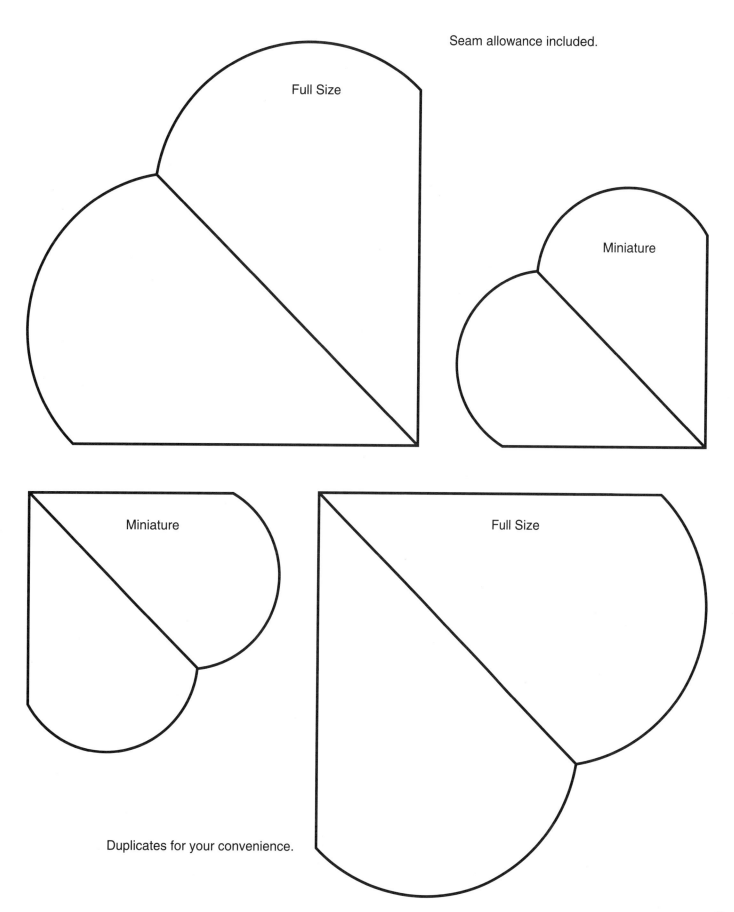

Seam allowance included.

Full Size

Miniature

Miniature

Full Size

Duplicates for your convenience.

16 Block Miniature Dutch Windmills

16 blocks
4 blocks across
4 blocks down

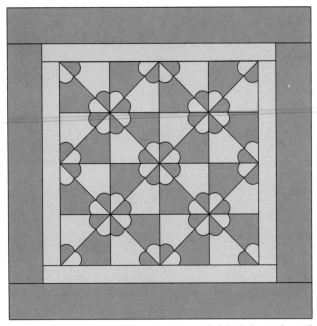

Approximate finished size 27" x 27"

Yardage & Cutting			*cut strips selvage to selvage*		
Fabric 1	1 yd	2	5½" wide strips		
			cut into	8	5½" squares
		1	8" wide strip		
			cut into	4	8" squares*
		4	2" wide strips for the border		
Fabric 2	1 yd	2	5½" wide strips		
			cut into	8	5½" squares
		1	8" wide strip		
			cut into	4	8" squares*
		4	3½" wide strips for the border		
Interfacing*	¾ yd	6	3½" wide strips		
			cut into	32	3½" squares
Backing	1 yd		36" x 36"		
Bonded Batting	1 yd		36" x 36"		
Binding	⅜ yd	3	3" wide strips		

Yardage figured on 42" wide fabric.
*Unnecessary if reusing "cut away" hearts.

There are two options for constructing the heart portion:

Option 1. Use the "cut away" portion of the heart left from making a larger quilt.

   or

Option 2. Make a pieced block for the heart.

If using the "cut away," be sure to test that the fusible separates easily from the "cut away" piece before beginning construction of your quilt. If the fusible does not easily peel away from the "heart" piece, you will need to purchase the additional fabric and fusible interfacing to create the smaller heart unit.

Making 16 Large Blocks

1. Follow the instructions on pages 20 through 24 to make 16 pieced blocks from the 5½" squares.

2. Square blocks to 5".

Quiltmakers who love the challenge of making miniature quilts will enjoy making a smaller version of "Dutch Windmills." The miniature block finishes at 4½" square.

Making 32 Heart Units, choose Option 1 or 2

Follow the instructions on page 26 to make the smaller sized template found on page 49.
Cut out the template very accurately on the marked line.

Option 1. Making the heart units using the "cut away" portions from your larger sized quilts

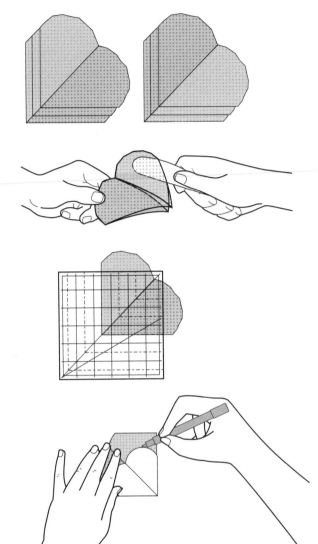

1. You need a total of 32 "cut away" hearts. Separate your "cut away" hearts in two equal stacks as shown. Be sure to have 16 of each kind.

2. Gently loosen the fusible interfacing from the pieced fabric heart, leaving the top of the arc attached to the background fabric.

3. Square each to 3½".

4. Lay the template on top of the "cut away" heart, with the interfacing smooth side up. Be sure to match the right angles.

5. Trace the curves of the template with a fine line permanent marker.

6. Repeat for all of the heart units.

Option 2. Making the heart units if not reusing the "cut away" hearts from a larger quilt

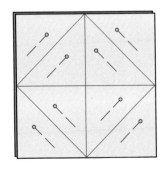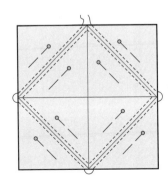

1. On the wrong side of the light fabric draw a light pencil line through the middle of the 8" by 8" square in both directions. Connect the drawn lines.

2. Place square of light and dark fabrics right sides together. Press and pin.

3. Sew a quarter inch from both sides of the diagonal line.

4. Press.

5. Cut apart on the pencil lines.

6. Press open toward the dark side.

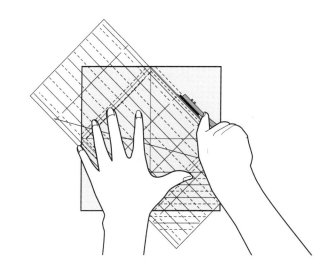

7. Square to 3½". You need a total of 32 pieced blocks for the hearts.

8. Arrange in two stacks of 16. Be sure they are turned correctly.

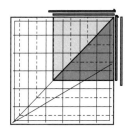

9. Lay 3½" interfacing square on pieced block, smooth side up. Be sure to match the right angles.

10. Trace the curves of the template with a fine line permanent marker.

11. Repeat for all heart units in each stack.

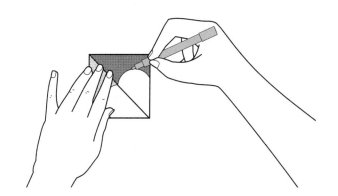

Appliqueing Hearts

Refer to applique techniques on pages 27 through 31.

Sewing the Blocks Together

Lay out and sew together blocks according to the baby quilt layout.

Adding the Mitered Borders

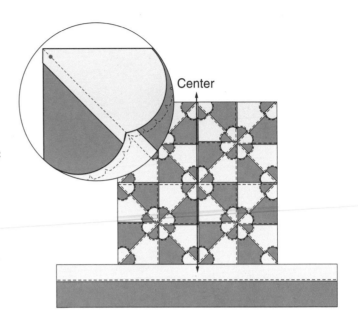

1. Mark a quarter inch dot on all four corners of your quilt.

2. Sew the light and dark border strips together.

3. Find the center of your quilt and match to the center of the border strips. Pin.

Center

4. Sew the border strips to your quilt, being sure to begin and end your sewing at the quarter inch mark.

5. Follow the directions for mitered borders found on page 39.

Finishing Your Quilt

Follow the directions for finishing your quilt on page 43.
Machine quilt in the ditch as shown.

Binding

Follow the directions for binding found on page 46.

Acknowledgements

A heartfelt thanks to the many students who challenged me with their wonderful ideas and creative input to my book.

Deepest thanks to the "storegirls" whose encouragement is so heartwarming. My thanks also to the whole QIAD family. Your support and kindness make this a second home for me. I love you all!

Special thanks to Loretta, Susan and Merritt, the creative geniuses I most depend on.

To Sue Bouchard, my dear friend, for coming up with the miniature "Dutch Windmills."

To Janet Raines, who gave me my start at QIAD. I love and miss you... come home soon!

And to Eleanor Burns who continues to inspire me and whom I treasure as both mentor and friend. I will be forever grateful for all you have given me.

Index

Order Information

Quilt in a Day books offer a wide range of techniques and are directed toward a variety of skill levels. If you do not have a quilt shop in your area, you may write for a complete catalog and current price list of all books and patterns published by Quilt in a Day®, Inc., 1955 Diamond Street, San Marcos, CA 92069 or call to order toll free 1 800 777-4852 between the hours of 8am – 5pm Pacific Time.

Easy

These books are easy enough for beginners of any age.
Log Cabin Quilt in a Day
Irish Chain Quilt
Bits & Pieces Quilt
Trip Around the World
Heart's Delight Wallhanging
Scrap Quilt
Rail Fence Quilt
Dresden Placemats
Flying Geese Quilt
Star for all Seasons Placemats
Winning Hand Quilt
Courthouse Steps Quilt
From Blocks to Quilt

Applique

While these books offer a variety of techniques, easy applique is featured in each.

Applique in a Day
Dresden Plate Quilt
Sunbonnet Sue Visits Quilt in a Day
Recycled Treasures
Country Cottages and More
Creating with Color
Spools & Tools Wallhanging
Dutch Windmills Quilt

Intermediate to Advanced

With a little Quilt in a Day experience, these books offer a rewarding project.
Trio of Treasured Quilts
Lover's Knot Quilt
Amish Quilt
May Basket Quilt
Morning Star Quilt
Friendship Quilt
Tulip Quilt
Star Log Cabin Quilt

Burgoyne Surrounded Quilt
Bird's Eye Quilt
Snowball Quilt
Tulip Table Runner

Holiday

When a favorite holiday is approaching, Quilt in a Day is there to help you plan.
Country Christmas
Bunnies & Blossoms
Patchwork Santa
Last Minute Gifts
Angel of Antiquity
Log Cabin Wreath Wallhanging
Log Cabin Tree Wallhanging
Country Flag
Lover's Knot Placemats

Sampler

Always and forever popular are books with a variety of patterns.
The Sampler
Block Party Series 1, Quilter's Year
Block Party Series 2, Baskets and Flowers
Block Party Series 3, Quilters' Almanac
Block Party Series 4, Christmas Traditions
Block Party Series 5, Pioneer Sampler

Angle Piecing

Quilt in a Day "template free" methods make angle cutting less of a challenge.
Diamond Log Cabin Tablecloth or Treeskirt
Pineapple Quilt
Blazing Star Tablecloth
Schoolhouse Quilt
Radiant Star Quilt

Templates

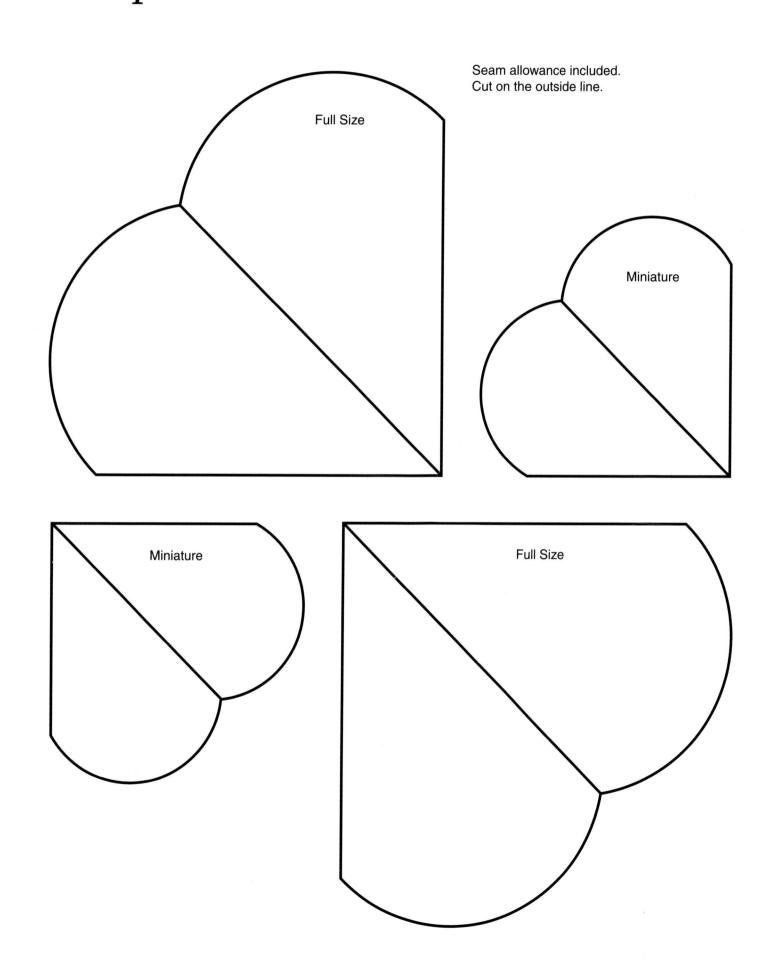

Full Size

Seam allowance included.
Cut on the outside line.

Miniature

Miniature

Full Size